ARIKA L. PIERCE

D0632023

THE MILLENNIAL'S PLAYBOOK TO ADULTING

ARIKA L. PIERCE

DOWNLOAD THE AUDIOBOOK FREE!

As a thank you for buying my book, I would like to give you the Audiobook version 100% FREE!
TO DOWNLOAD GO TO:
www.arikapierce.com

DEDICATION

I would like to dedicate this book to the following people:

My grandparents

To James Sr. & Maudella Pierce and Earl & Rosie Johnson – I am a firm believer that everything starts at the top. The determination each of you had to ensure that our lives were easier than yours is felt every day and that blessing is never lost on me.

My parents

Thank you for always encouraging me to pursue my dreams. From when I wanted to be a hairdresser, lawyer, beauty queen, and jewelry designer, your support has never wavered, and I would not be the person I am today without both of you (or technically alive ;-)
To say I love you and thank you is not enough.

My big sister

Adey, you are my biggest supporter, cheerleader and protector. I could not have picked a better big sister (well besides Oprah) to be on my team for life.

Thank you for always catching me when I fall and having the *champs* ready when I succeed. At the end of the day I am still a little sister who adores her big sister. #thepiercesisters

My family & friends

I am blessed with more family and friends than I could possibly name. Words can't properly express how thankful I am for all of the support, encouragement and love each of you give me. It takes a village!

My personal advisory board

To Fred, Dean Robinson, and Maria – each of you has been instrumental at different points in my life, probably to a degree that you may not realize. Thank you for believing in and guiding me.

My three favorite millennials

To Jarron, TJ, and MJ – you three were the inspiration for this book. Thank you for letting me be your honorary big sister. I am proud of each of you and can't wait to see the amazing things you do. If you ever need ANYTHING, you know where to find me. And text/DM me from time to time!

Contents

Dear Universe: I missed the How to Be an Adult 101 Class.

Send Help.
And My Mom.
And Wine.

Introduction

Adulting is Such a Blast: Said no one ever. A few years ago, a millennial interned at my firm. While working with him, I realized that many day-to-day work activities I practiced without thinking were new territories for him. I knew his intelligence was not the issue and eventually learned it was a skills issue. No one had taught him how to work with and function professionally and socially with older generations. No one had taught him the basics of functioning as an adult in an adult-dominated world. I remember thinking, "well, how the hell would he know to put a subject line in every email— he only sends texts and DMs." It was this *aha!* moment that inspired me to create this playbook so that millennials can be better prepared for adulthood and positively accepted by older generations instead of everyone constantly complaining about the millennial generation.

If you are reading this book, my guess is that you might be a millennial who needs a little (or a lot) of direction in navigating adult life and could use some play-by-play tips for "successful" adulting (if there is such a thing). My observation over the past few years is that millennials get negatively stereotyped. Everyone complains about them, and there are lots of books and articles written on how to work with millennials, talk to millennials and manage millennials, but very few one-stop sources made *for* millennials to quickly capture some life guidelines that may have skipped over the millennial generation. And that's what I want this book to be.

This playbook will help make you a successful (or at least semi-successful) adult. The book is short, the chapters are quick, and the info is straightforward. My ultimate goal is to give you the info that everyone complains about millennials not knowing, but no one seems to be taking the time to teach or share.

You may be asking what's makes me the "millennial expert"? I'm actually what is known as an Xennial (yes, it is a real term, google it). I was born in March 1980, so I'm right on the cusp of Generation X and millennial. Being an Xennial means that even though I graduated from college almost 20 years ago and I have a career, a mortgage, and lots of other 'adult-like' things, I still relate and identify with millennials (i.e., going down IG rabbit holes is my favorite past time, and I can't imagine life without having everything from my wine to my paper towels delivered to me by pushing a button on my phone). Also, over the past 15 years, I have learned a lot about this thing called "adulting" the hard way, and throughout this book, I will share some of those stories so that you don't make some of the same mistakes I did. Does this book have all the answers? No—but I try to touch on what I think are some of the most important aspects of adulting, such as creating your personal brand, finding a job, keeping a job, and even staying mentally, physically and financially fit. My hope is that you actually: (1) read to the end and, (2) take 1-2 of these tips and use them to become the best adult you can be. That's my challenge to you. Now let's get this adult thing started!

You are the CEO of Me Inc. and the Chief Marketing Officer for the brand called You.

Chapter 1 :

Breaking Out of the Millennial Brand

Brands matter. And your personal brand should matter to you because it is how someone would describe you when you are not there. A few years ago, whenever my friends would say things like "that's not really aligned with my brand," I would laugh and remind them that the last time I checked their last name was not Kardashian or Carter[1], so I wasn't aware that they had a "brand" to protect. Now, I'm the one who makes those types of comments because I have learned that, in today's world, we ALL have a personal brand that needs to be created and protected.

You may have started to establish your brand through the organizations you've joined, jobs or internships you may have had, or advocacy on issues that are important to you. Some of you may not yet have an established brand identity or may have one that has gone in the wrong direction. No matter what stage you are in, you still have the power to control how you are known both professionally and personally. What is most important is that you maintain this control as you embark on your career because one wrong move

---

[1] Mr. and Mrs. Shawn Carter aka Jay and Bey

can impact everything you have worked hard for over the past few years. If you don't believe you need a brand, keep in mind that the moment you walk through the doors of your first job, you have a brand that has been given to you by others. Also, as a millennial your brand can already be in need of some repair work, as many will assume you have a "me, me, me" mentality and that you are lazy, entitled, and in need of instant gratification.[2] While some of these traits may be true, these are not characteristics you want to be known for as you enter the workforce. So, let's do something about it.

How Millennials Are Described in One Word

Entitled, Impatient, Tech-Obsessed, Pampered, Self-Absorbed, Lazy

---

Think about how you want your co-workers or your boss to speak about you to other people. For

---

[2] If you haven't seen the *Sponsor a Millennial Today* YouTube video, take 5 minutes to watch it. Yes, this is what people think of you.

me, I have always wanted people to know me professionally as a hard worker, dependable and someone who will get the job done. This is as important to me as being branded as being smart because I know a lot of smart people who have zero work ethic (which makes them less than smart). Take time right now to think about what you want to be known for as you start your career. How do you want people to describe you when you are not there? Are you a team player? A strong writer? Energetic? A natural leader? Or are you difficult to work with? Someone who requires a lot of hand-holding? Timid? Also, when a potential employer googles you, what comes up? These are all considerations when building out a positive brand image.

ASSIGNMENT

Write down three words or phrases that you would like your current co-workers or future co-workers to use to describe you.

Once you know how you want to be perceived professionally, think about what will need to be done to earn this reputation. Someone who is consistently late or turns in work with typos is not going to have a reputation of being reliable or detail-orientated. A person who is constantly on Instagram or Snapchatting from their desk is not going to be seen as someone who is taking their career seriously, focused or a go-getter. As you go throughout your day, keep in mind that people are watching you and to be 100% honest, because you are a millennial, many are waiting for you to fail due to the negative perceptions of the generation. It is up to you to create a brand that proves these stereotypes wrong. Surprise and shock people and be the millennial that rises to the top. Build a reputation that conveys that you will show up (on time), do the work, and are eager to learn.

For example, when you get an assignment, don't be afraid to ask for background on where your work fits into a bigger part of the project. It can show that you are someone that has a real interest in the work and a desire to be a part of the team and not just a task rabbit. Also, when it's time for a performance review with your boss, tell them that as someone new to the workforce, you would like to know how they would describe you professionally and ask how they have heard others describe you. Not only will this provide you with key feedback on the direction of your brand and reputation, but it will also show them that you are taking the early stages of your career seriously, which shows a level of maturity that will make you stand out from your other millennial peers.

Your brand is what people say about you when you are not in the room.

– Jeff Bezos, CEO of Amazon (and the earth's wealthiest person)

Social Media

Over the years, I have reviewed resumes and interviewed millennials for their first or second job out of college. I always google the applicant's name and search for them on social media to see what comes up. I'm always impressed when I find a LinkedIn profile with at least a semi-professional headshot[3] and social media accounts that are private and not viewable to the public. I find it shocking when someone doesn't have enough judgment to restrict access to an Instagram page full of them smoking weed or twerking half-naked in a pool in Miami. And let me be clear, I don't think it's your employer's business what you do in your personal time, but I *do* think an employer has the right to question what type of professional judgment you may have based on how you decide to protect your personal life. For example, I know many people who will not even interview someone who has social media posts that contain outspoken political views and polarizing statements. It may not be right, but just know these are the types of things employers are now doing as they screen applicants and weed out poor brands. Whether or not it's fair is irrelevant—it happens.

---

[3] If there is a red cup in your hand it is not semi-professional

---

ASSIGNMENT

Google yourself, and identify anything online that could negatively impact your "brand."

Also, be careful about what you post about colleagues and especially your boss online. One of my friends recently stumbled onto the Facebook page of one of his employees, and it was filled with negative posts about how much he hated his boss (my friend) and how he turned his work computer at an angle so he could 'Netflix and chill' all day at work. His employment was short-lived.

The bottom line is that no matter how much of a great job you do of creating a positive brand reputation for yourself, it can quickly be ruined by your digital presence. Some items on the internet you may not have control over, such as legal documents or a mug shot, but you absolutely have control over who can view and judge your social media accounts. If you want your private life to stay private, change your settings and keep them private.

If keeping your social media accounts open to the public is important you, I recommend scrubbing them of any incriminating photos or negative status updates. In some industries, the right type of social media feed can actually be helpful and enhance your brand (for example, if you are a graphic designer, having an Instagram page that shows your work can be positive for your brand). In this instance, create a second account that is public but separate and distinct from your personal account (which would be private). The key is to show that you have good judgment and professional maturity to know what is appropriate for public consumption and what is not.

Things Your Employer Does Not Want to See About You Online

- Inappropriate or provocative photos
- Photos with drugs or excessive alcohol use
- Discriminatory comments
- Comments insulting a colleague or a previous employer
- Highly unprofessional screennames
- Anything linked to criminal activity or behavior
- Confidential information that belongs to a former or current employer
- Extreme political views

Takeaways

Your brand matters and will be given to you by others.

As a millennial, certain negative assumptions will be made about you, so it is important to prove these characteristics wrong.

Live your best life on social media but be smart about it.

Live up to the reputation YOU set for yourself!

Never Stop Believing That Somewhere Someone Is Looking for Exactly What You Have to Offer.

Chapter 2:

Swiping Left (for a Job)

Ask any millennial what one of the hardest parts of adulting is, and most would say finding the right job. It's a lot like finding the right date online; you have to do a lot of swiping left before you finally match with someone else who has swiped right.

I could write a whole book on finding a job, resume tips, workplace etiquette, etc. For now, I am going to focus on the *most* important tools at this early stage of your career. However, if you want more information on this topic check out my website[4] for future workshops, webinars, and in-person seminars where I will go deeper into the job search process. Knowing how to find and land the right job is a major key (in my DJ Khaled voice) to success, and for some crazy reason, they don't always give you these tools in college.

Resume

Hopefully, you already have a resume. If not, don't panic! It's ok, but get working on one ASAP. Even in today's digital world, a resume is what gets you in the door. They are still the way most employers vet applicants. Making sure yours stands

---

[4] Shameless plug for www.arikapierce.com

out from the rest is important in securing the first goal of the job hunt—an interview. There are plenty of online resources that can help you develop a resume, so I am not going to spend a lot of time on the basics.[5] Instead, I want to share with you five tips to ensure you have a five-star resume—some I learned the hard way.

1. **Your resume should be one page.** I've been in the workforce for almost 20 years, and my resume is two pages, so I'm shocked when I get a resume from someone who is embarking on their first job and has a 3-4 page resume. Usually, it's because they are not formatting efficiently or the job descriptions are dissertation-length rather than short bulleted summaries. Unless you are a child prodigy who started working while in elementary school, take a look at what can be done to get it to one page. Keep it relevant.

2. **Formatting counts**. A resume should be easy to read. Little things like lines and bullets to organize the info and using easy to read fonts can go a long way to helping you stand

---

[5] There are also services that will review your resume and/or redo your resume. One to check out is Layfield Resume Consulting, www.layfieldresume.com

out—especially when an employer is bombarded with a bunch of resumes. If given a choice between a resume that looks succinct and easy to read and one which looks like a term paper, the succinct one will win every time.

3. **NO TYPOS**. Yes, a no-brainer, but you would be surprised how many typos I have seen in resumes—including my own! One of my most embarrassing interviews was with a panel of three partners at a fancy law firm; one of the partners pointed out to me (in front of everyone) that I had two typos on my resume. I definitely did not get the job, but as a result, I always triple check any changes I make to my resume. Details matter.

4. **Always email your resume in a PDF**. A PDF ensures that the resume you created on your computer is not screwed up on its way to the potential employer's email inbox. Because some people are using Macs and some are using PCs, and everyone is using a different version of Word, version control is important. I can't tell you how many times I have opened an applicant's resume (especially from my phone) and because I use a Mac, it looks all

crazy on my screen. They could be a perfect candidate, but I'm already turned off—next!

5. **It's time for a professional email address**. If your email is thesearebloodyshoes6969@gmail.com, you will not get an interview. Enough said.

How to Look for a Job

Now that your resume is PDF'd and ready to go, let's talk about looking for a job. My advice is: if you don't have a job, you should look for one like it is your full-time job. I repeat, look for a job like it's your full-time job! This means setting targets and hitting them until it's your first day of work. Job searching is partly a numbers game. The more jobs you apply for, the higher the odds are that you will get one. I'm blown away by someone who doesn't have a job (and wants one) but is passively applying to 1-2 jobs a week. If you are searching for a job, set a target of how many you want to apply for each day or week. A good number is 3-5 per day or 15-20 per week. Yes, it's a lot, especially when it comes to creating customized cover letters, but it's the only way to get in the groove. Whenever someone tells me they have been applying for jobs but haven't heard anything back, my first question is, "How many resumes are you sending out a week?" You must be aggressive and actively hunting for a job that fits your career goals. Apply, apply, apply.

TIP

While job hunting, keep a chart of the jobs you have applied for (you don't want to apply for the same job twice accidentally). Track things such as the company, job title, job listing, date you applied, contact details, interview notes, communications, etc. This will help you stay on top of what jobs you have applied for, next steps as well as track whether you are hitting your weekly targets.

The Power of LinkedIn

The next question I ask a job-seeker are "Where are you looking for jobs?" and "Do you have a LinkedIn profile?" Before you blow off LinkedIn (I used to as well), know that it is a powerful tool for both your professional brand and job search. It's only useless if you don't use it properly. Is it as much fun as Snapchat? No. But will it help you get a job? Yes. So, where you do you start?

1. **Create a LinkedIn profile.** If you don't have one already, set up an account (using your professional email address), and create a profile. This should not take you long as it's just the process of taking the items from your resume and putting them in the LinkedIn data fields. Also, I have increasingly seen those who are looking for jobs also upload their resume to their profile. Bottom line, recruiters look at LinkedIn—make sure your profile looks professional, is up to date, and is clear about the type of job you're looking for. (Tip: spend some time on your headline to make it appropriately standout with the right keywords)

2. **Upload a legit picture.** This is a MUST, and it is imperative that your picture coveys your professional brand—this is not the time or place for your favorite Instagram selfie. If you don't have a

professional headshot (which you probably do not), put on a professional outfit and groom yourself as if you were going to a job interview. Tailor your backdrop to the type of job you are targeting. For example, if you are looking for an office/corporate job stand in front of a neutral wall, or if you are in the creative or artistic field, a brighter or motion background may be more appropriate. Use your best judgment and have someone snap a few pictures that you can turn into a headshot with some snazzy editing. Studies have shown that applicants with a professional profile picture stand out from applicants with no pictures or ones that have a profile but the picture looks like it was taken at happy hour.

3. **Make connections**. After your profile is set up, this is where the fun starts. It's time to engage and interact. Start joining networking groups such as your college alumni groups and groups affiliated with your major, interests or job field. Follow leaders and influencers that you find

interesting, and don't be afraid to send a connection request to people you know or would like to know. If you can't find a single person to connect with, start with me.[6] (I promise to accept.) Your goals should be to build and solidify connections that can help in your job search.

4. **Publish something, share something.** One of the best features about LinkedIn is that it is a content platform. If you check out my LinkedIn, you will see that I periodically write and post original content on various topics that will help elevate my brand profile. It is self-serving and self-promotional, and I am ok with that. Also, share content that is posted by others as this will help you to solidify new connections.

5. **Look around.** LinkedIn is a great place to look for job openings and research companies where you have applied (or want to work). Check out employees who work there now, and even send a

---

[6] www.linkedin.com/in/arikapierce

connection request to the HR manager. If your account looks good, they likely will be impressed that you are such a proactive millennial and you will stand out and shine bright like a damn diamond.

TIP

Need to Upgrade Your LinkedIn?
Google "2017 Smart Personal Branding with LinkedIn" and read this eBook.

LinkedIn Disclaimer: People can tell when you've looked at their profile (so stalk with caution).

Finding a Job

Now that your LinkedIn profile is set up and you have your target number of jobs to apply for each week, it's time to get down to job hunting. Believe it or not, back in the day, you had to buy a newspaper and search the employment section for ads, *mail* a cover letter and resume to jobs, and wait for a phone call or rejection letter to show up in the mailbox (clutch your pearls). I tell you this so that you know how much easier the process is now. Here is the quick and dirty of the job hunt.

1. Identify websites that post the kind of jobs you want. One of my favorite sites is www.indeed.com. It's a search engine that combines job listings from thousands of websites and puts them in all one place. You can also set up alerts based on keywords, and they will email you daily listings of jobs that match your search terms. Other places are college job boards, trade associations for the field you're in (for example, if you are looking for a job in PR, check out the careers' page on the Public Relations Society of America website). LinkedIn is also a great resource. In addition to their job board, people post jobs in the groups. Lastly, if there is a company you are *dying* to work for, but they don't have any job openings available, don't be afraid to reach out to someone there and ask for an "informational interview." This is where you go in and ask questions to learn more

ARIKA L. PIERCE

about the company and tell them about yourself with the hope that if a job is made available, they will contact you. These don't always work, but as you wait for interview requests to come in, they are a great way to get some interview training.

2. When you are ready to apply for a job there are a couple of things to know:

    a. Read the application instructions carefully and FOLLOW them. (Remember this is your first test on whether you know how to follow directions!) Some will require just a cover letter and resume; some may ask for references or give you a specific subject line for your email. Whatever it is, don't mess it up by not paying attention to the details.

    b. If a cover letter is requested, you need a customized cover letter for every job you apply for. The best way to do this is to have a standard cover letter but tweak it as if you wrote it specifically for this job (i.e., insert why you want to work for *that* company, why the position matches well with your skill set, etc.). In my experience, cover letters are best received in a PDF attachment verses in the body of an email. Many HR people who screen your application will need to pass them along to the business leaders over the position for which you're applying. It's much easier to transfer that information if it's all sent in a PDF format.

c. Before you send out the application, triple check that everything is accurate. The last thing you want to do is send over a cover letter to your dream job with the wrong company or name listed. Also, make sure you are following the application instructions to a T! And, of course, don't forget to include the required attachments.

d. Press send, and repeat.

Major Keys

1. If you are applying for a job on a site like Indeed, never rely on them to create your resume by entering your info into the data fields—it looks horrible. In fact, I always delete these applications because, to me, it shows that the applicant took the shortcut, and it wasn't worth their time to send a real application. Always upload your resume (in the PDF) and still send over a customized cover letter. It will look like you took the process more seriously.

2. If you apply for a job through LinkedIn's "Easy Apply" and are really excited about the job, I suggest creating a customized cover letter to convey your interest in the company and create a single PDF with both your resume and cover letter. Also, if you want to go a step further, send the person who posted the job a note introducing yourself. If the person is getting hundreds of applications, both of these extra steps will make you stand out from what could be hundreds of resumes. The worst thing that could happen is that they ignore you (or on the positive side, they want to interview you!).

3. After you have applied, it's a waiting game, which is why it's important to keep repeating the process until you are officially hired—I repeat: do not stop this process until you have an *official* job offer. I know of countless examples of people who thought they had a job, so they quit looking only for that job to fall through.

4. Check your email and voicemail. I know that email and voicemail is something mostly *older* people do (i.e., people over 40). But I can almost guarantee that it is highly unlikely that you will get a text or a DM requesting that you come in for an interview. That means it's time to start checking your email *multiple* times a day. If a potential employer emails you on a Tuesday to request an interview and you don't get back to them until Friday, they will assume you aren't serious about the position. Be prompt with your responses. The same goes for voicemail. If your mailbox is full, they can't leave a message to offer you an interview (or job), and it is highly unlikely they are going to call you back.

TIP

Just like your email address, it's also vital that your voicemail message be professional. This is not the time for funny antics—use the automated message or create a simple voicemail that sounds like you—smart and professional (and in need of a job!).

Job interviews are like first dates. Good impressions count. Awkwardness can occur. Outcomes are unpredictable.

The Interview

As I said before, job hunting is a lot like online dating, you have to keep at it, and eventually, something will stick. The interview is pretty much the first date and will determine whether there will be a second date. So, get excited this is the time to shine! Here are some tips to prep for the interview:

1. Make sure you are clear on the date, time, location, etc. of the interview. This is not the time to "figure it out later" or be "clutch."

2. Do some additional research on the company, the position, the person or people you will be meeting or speaking with (if it's a phone interview). Has the company been in the news lately? Did the person you are interviewing with go to your college?

3. Come up with 3-5 questions to ask them. There is nothing worse than when an interview candidate is asked if they have any questions and their response is either "No" or "Will I be able to work from home?" It's much better to say something like, "I was doing some research on the company and I read X, and want to ask Y." One of my go-to questions

is, "How will you measure the success of the person in this position?"

4. If you aren't experienced in interviewing, do some role-playing (the clean kind!). Have a friend or family member play the role of the interviewer and practice as if it's the real thing. A few basic questions that you are likely to be asked are:

    a. Can you tell me a little bit more about yourself?

    b. Why do you want to work here?

    c. What interested you most about this position?

    d. Why should we hire you?

    e. What do you expect to see yourself doing in 5 to 10 years?

5. Print some hard copies of your resume on high-quality paper. It may seem old school, but the moment during the interview when the interviewer is scrambling to find your resume under a stack of papers or in their inbox, and you pull out a nice and crisp resume from your bag, they will be impressed.

Interview Day

So, it's interview day. This should go without saying, but ARRIVE EARLY. They will not care if your Uber canceled or the subway was delayed. Factor everything that might go wrong and get to the interview 10-15 minutes before it's supposed to start. I cannot stress this enough. Again, remember from Chapter 1, this is your brand! You don't want to be known for arriving late to your interview—they will never forget it. Of course, sometimes things happen that you can't control. I have a friend who was in a car accident on her way to a job interview. In addition to calling to inform the company she would not make it, she went the extra step and sent a same-day Edible Arrangements as an apology/thank you for them setting aside the time to speak with her with a little "I hope I haven't thrown a monkey wrench in your plans" note. They called her the next day, insisted she reschedule the interview, and ultimately she got the job! The lesson here is, if something happens out of your control, go above and beyond to rectify the situation. It never hurts and can help a lot. At least send a note or something!

As far as what to wear, while there may be a few exceptions, you should be dressed in business attire. For men, this means wearing either a suit or slacks with a blazer. DO NOT WEAR JEANS. I REPEAT DO NOT WEAR JEANS. Even if you are told, "we are a casual office you do not have to dress up," do not take that as a green light to wear jeans. The same goes for women. Wear a suit, a work-appropriate dress (if you have ever worn it to a club, it's probably not work appropriate), or a pair of pants (leggings do not count) with a blazer.

While we will dive deeper into appearance in Chapter Four, use your best judgment to look the part. I was once helping someone prep for an interview and suggested that he shave his Rick Ross-esque beard before the interview unless he was interviewing at Maybach Music (he was not). He shaved and was upset after the interview because the man he interviewed with had a beard. I explained that even so, the difference between the two of them was that the man doing the interview already had a job and he did not.

Interview Tips

1. Arrive early. (It's worth repeating).
2. Look the part.
3. Make sure your phone is turned off.

4. Be nice and gracious to the receptionist and anyone else you come into contact with while you are there. Hopefully, this is natural for you. If it isn't, practice some manners and know that every interaction you have is part of the interview process.

5. When you are introduced to the person or people you are interviewing with, shake their hands and look them in the eyes. Show confidence (even if you have to fake it!).

6. Listen to the questions you are asked and don't be afraid to take a few moments to think about your response. If you don't understand the question, say so or ask the interviewer to repeat it.

7. Don't forget to ask your questions and drop in something to reflect that you have researched the company.

8. Ask about next steps. This is as simple as saying something like, "May I ask where are you in the hiring process?" or "Can I ask about the timing, in terms of when you would like to have someone hired?"

TIP

If you get offered a job during the interview, it may seem like a dream come true and feel flattering, but know it is not typical and could be a red flag about the company or organization. Even though your interview skills may be amazing, you should question why the company is so desperate to hire someone so quickly. In this situation, I would kindly thank them for the offer and ask if you can get back to them within the next 24 hours.

Post Interview

Let me tell you a quick story. When I was about 23, I was interviewing for what I thought was going to be my dream job. I went in for three different interviews and was fairly confident that I would be joining their team. At the third and final interview, I was told it was down to two candidates and that they would let me know their decision in a few days. Well, it was to my surprise when I received an email thanking me for my time and, while I was an outstanding candidate, they had made an offer to the other candidate (insert cry emoji). After I picked myself up from the feeling of rejection (told you the process is just like dating), I reached out to my sister who encouraged me to write back and thank them for letting me know and ask for feedback on my interviews (since I was new to this). I sent the email, and the hiring manager actually called me. She explained how the other candidate and I were pretty much equal (she gave me the, "if we could have hired both of you we would have" line). But the major difference between us was that after each of the three interviews the other candidate sent a thank you note to everyone she interviewed with, and I had sent none. So, in the end, they went with her. (I guess her brand was seen as more polite!)

I can't tell you how upset I was with myself. I didn't get the job because of a *f-ing* thank you note? I was shocked, disappointed and really angry. BUT it's a mistake that I have never made again and I remind the hell out of everyone I know who is interviewing to send a thank you note—and yes, email is just fine. Just send it. Also, if you don't get a job, ask for feedback on how you interviewed and for any advice they could give you as you continue your job hunt. The story about the (non) thank you note happened 15 years ago and continues to be one of the best pieces of career advice I've ever received.

The last thing to know about the interview process is that, just like dating, if you are interested in "going out again" the waiting sucks. This is one of the reasons it's important to ask about next steps during the interview, so you have an idea of when to expect to hear back from the employer. Sometimes, they may respond to your thank you note, and sometimes they may "ghost you," and you'll never hear from them again. I recommend waiting for 8-10 days post interview and following-up if you haven't heard anything. A short email saying you are just checking in to see how things are progressing is fine and it also reinforces that you remain interested in the position. I don't recommend this technique in dating ☺

Phone or Virtual Interviews

On many occasions, your first interview with a prospective employer may be a phone interview. Sometimes, this is just a way for the employer to screen you without you having to get all fancy and come into their office. I encourage you to apply all of the previous tips as if it is in person, down to putting on work-appropriate clothing to do the phone interview (especially if it is a virtual interview) and sending a thank you note. It may sound crazy, but when you are dressed professionally, you will convey professionalism even through the phone. It's the same reason why they tell people who work from home to not work in their pajamas. Here are a few additional tips for phone or virtual interviews:

1. Take the interview from a quiet space, and ensure your phone or computer has a strong connection. This is not the time to step outside of happy hour or the gym to take a call.

2. For virtual interviews, make a test call and make sure you have your phone or computer set up in the right position to see you (i.e., your prospective employer will not want to be staring up your nose for 30 minutes).
3. Don't multi-task. Turn off all distractions—social media, video games, tv, etc. You want to pretend you are sitting in front of that person and give them your full attention.

What About the Money

My first job out of college I was told I would be paid $24,000 the first six months and then a whopping 1K increase to a grand total of $25,000. The funny thing is, after the first six months I didn't see an increase in my paycheck, and I didn't have the courage to ask where my extra $38 was each paycheck. Being young and overly agreeable, I never drummed up the courage to ask, "What about my raise that we discussed?" This was a terrible mistake—being clear about your financial expectations is crucial.

I will give you this advice. It's perfectly ok to ask during an interview for a salary range for the position. Unless it's volunteer work, it's important to know whether the salary will work for you. While I would not make it the first question out of your mouth, I would ensure you have a sense of how much is on the table by the first or second interview. You don't want a situation when a job offer finally comes in, and it's below the poverty level. That's a waste of your and the employer's time.

A new job is like a blank book, and you are the author.

YOU GOT THE JOB!!!

Before you start popping bottles, let's take care of some business first.

1. When you get the call or email offering you the job, be very gracious, but ask if you can have 24-48 hours to get back to them. Why? During this time, you should evaluate if there are any other opportunities that you have interviewed for and are also interested in (this is when the tracking chart will come in handy). If you have any opportunities that fall in this category, send an email stating that you remain very interested in the position but have received a job offer and are hoping to get an update on where they are in the hiring process. This is also the time to do some math (you should know the official salary at this time) and understand if both the money and the job work for you. Take a day or two to think things over before accepting. If they need an immediate answer, well that changes things—but most employers should be able to give you some time to sleep on it.

2. Ask for an offer letter. They may be surprised that you even know to ask for this, but essentially this will be a letter that not only

outlines the position title and salary but also start date, benefits, vacation days, hours, etc.

3. Understand your benefits package. For example, when does your health insurance start? Does the company offer things such as tuition reimbursement? Commuting or parking benefits? Your salary is only part of your benefits package, so be familiar with the other ways you'll be compensated.

4. Once you accept an offer, be very clear on your:
   a. Start date
   b. What time you should arrive
   c. Who you should ask for when you arrive on your first day
   d. If there is anything you should read or review before you start
   e. What you should bring with you on the first day
   f. Ask if there is anything you should know about your first day/week

It's the First Day of ~~School~~ Work

The day is finally here. After sending who knows how many resumes, getting very few responses, and surviving the interview process, it is finally the FIRST DAY! Remember, your brand with your boss and colleagues starts *now*, so it's important to show up ready to "do the work" (don't worry, that's the next chapter!!). First, let me just give you a few tips on how to kick ass on the first day.

1. **Arrive early**. Don't be the stereotypical millennial who shows up late the first day of work with a Starbucks cup in hand.
2. **Dress the part**. Much like your interview, even if you are told to dress casually, do not wear jeans on your first day. Trust me—it's always best to just play it safe.[7]
3. **Make sure you have all of the documents you need**. The first day is usually spent doing paperwork. A lot of this paperwork is tied to getting paid, so it's in your best interest to make sure you can take care of this on day one. Otherwise, you may see your first pay period come and go without getting paid.
4. **Bring a notebook and a pen, and actually use it**. I know it sounds old school, but when you are sitting in your new boss' office and they start rattling off info, you will need somewhere to write down the important stuff they are saying. The notes app on your phone is not the place and your computer may not

---

[7] Check out my story on page 82

be set up yet or may be out of reach (i.e., at your desk).

5. **If someone asks you to go to lunch, say yes.** These are the people who you will be spending hours with each day. Developing personal relationships will be crucial to understanding the personalities of your new work environment.

6. **Smile, relax, and enjoy the first day of 40+ years of working!!**

TIP

Self-audit your resume and LinkedIn profile (even if you already have a job) to identify where improvements can be made, and make them within one week.

The only place success comes before work is in the dictionary.

Chapter 3:

Doing the Work (25 Ways to Stay Employed)

I've been working since I was 14. The only time I have not had a job was my first year of law school because it was not allowed. I've never been fired from a job or even received a poor performance review. What's my secret? I do the work. This has been my favorite chapter to write because millennials have a reputation of having a sense of entitlement and are unwilling to pay their dues in the early days because they want to skip right to being the boss. This may work for some, but it's rare. This chapter consists of my 25 tips on how to do the work, which will not just result in you staying gainfully employed, but pave the way for promotions, salary increases, and overall professional growth.

1. **Set Three Goals**. In your first week (if not first day) of any new job, always establish your top three goals for your new job. Perhaps your goals could include building a skill set or leading a project. Whatever they are, identify them early on and make sure you are working towards them daily. This will position you for success from day one.

2. **Be on time.** Arrive on time, and unless your boss is a crazy workaholic, I advise not leaving

before your boss. If you do, always stop by their office to say goodbye and confirm that they don't need anything else for the day. Also, if you are going to be late, let your boss know *before* you are late. Additionally, always give advanced notice if you are leaving early (and put it on any shared calendars). If your start time is 9 am and you email or text your boss at 9:15 am to say that you are going to be late, you are telling them what they already know. Bottom line, if you are entry-level (having limited experience), show off the things you have direct control over, like being on time. Note, this also applies to meetings, conference calls, etc. Be on time for everything.

3. **START work on time**. Yes, this is different from being on time. For example, if your start time is 9 am, then at 9 am you should be at your desk and ready to work. That means if you like to get coffee, catch up with co-workers, eat breakfast, etc., before you start working, factor all of that into your schedule and get to work early to account for this time. Your new employer is likely not going to be excited to pay for you to be standing in the

Starbucks line when you should be at your desk working (unless you are getting him or her coffee).

4. **Get a company mentor**. This person is not your boss but can work for your company. In a perfect world you should actually have a mentor who works for the same employer and one who does not. I'll go deeper into this in Chapter 6. Regardless, it will be important to have someone who you can go to with questions, ideas, and sometimes even tears (though I do **not** recommend crying at work) about your work life, career goals, etc.

5. **Write $hit down**. Everyone has a different way of storing info, but my foolproof method is that I keep a notebook where I write EVERYTHING down in one place (yes, another old-school moment). I keep a to-do list, notes from meetings, conference calls, conversations with my boss, etc. all in the same notebook, and I probably go through three to four notebooks a year. Even if you transfer things to an electronic method, it's always good to have a central notebook within reach because, unlike college, you will be in many situations (like sitting in a meeting

or in your boss' office) where you might not have quick access to a computer or tablet. And nothing says unprepared like having to ask your boss for a pen and paper or walking out of their office and already forgetting what they just asked you to do. When all else fails, write it down. Leaving everything to marinate in your brain is a quick and easy way to forget and fail.

6. **Be your own project manager**. I recently heard on the podcast Paychecks & Balances[8] (a great one to check out if you haven't already) the advice to keep a central tracking document (excel spreadsheets, Trello, or whatever works best for you) of any and all ongoing projects. The tracking document should include items such as the project/task description, estimated due date, target date, completed date, and priority (low, medium, high). Even if your boss doesn't request that you do it, keep this document for yourself and send it to them weekly as a courtesy (you will get you SO many extra points for this). Remember, in this new *adult* world it's up to

---

[8] https://paychecksandbalances.com

you to manage your workload. Also, this will help you when it's time for performance reviews and in updating your resume with key projects on which you worked. All of your accomplishments will be right there in the tracking document.

7. **Do what you are asked to do**. Few people want the job of a professional coffee gopher, but in the early days of your career, there may be some shit work that you have to do. If you feel you are being taken advantage of, talk to your mentor, but sometimes this is just called "paying your dues." Show that you can handle more and the more substantive work should come.

8. **Stay abreast of what's going on with your company**. Read press releases, internal emails, earnings call transcripts (if the company is publically traded). Follow your company's social media accounts. Know what is going on with the company or organization outside of your cubicle or desk.

9. **Your calendar is your lifeline.** Put everything work-related on your work calendar: meetings, conference calls, deadlines, reminders, etc. This will ensure

you don't drop the ball by relying on your memory (again, I promise it will fail you at some point).

10. **Manage your work communications.** Email is usually the primary communication platform for companies (though some companies are also now using platforms such as Slack, Telegram, and even texts). Regardless of what it is—STAY ON TOP OF IT. Don't let days go by before you respond to emails and even if you are cc'd on an email, read it and keep up with what's going on. Also, learn to organize your communications with folders, sub-folders, etc. Don't be the employee with 947 unopened emails.

11. **Stay off your phone.** There is nothing worse than the millennial who spends more time on Snapchat during the day than working. Your phone is your own worst enemy at work. And yes, your boss can see when you stuff it quickly under your desk when he or she walks by.

12. **Ask questions.** Don't make assumptions or feel embarrassed to ask questions. You will save time if you ask early as opposed to

asking after the fact and doing an assignment or project wrong.

13. **Assume every email you send could be made public.** You do not own your work email domain. At any point, someone could be reading your email or forwarding it to someone it was not intended for. I've seen it happen time and time again. It is imperative that you keep work emails professional, you proofread before you hit send and avoid the OMGs, emojis, and unnecessary exclamation points!!!!!! Limit personal email on your work email, including office gossip, inappropriate language, etc. No work email is ever gone forever.

TIP

A lot of companies have email tracking systems in place that will flag your email if it contains profanity or references to drugs, violence, etc. Bottom line, big brother is watching.

---

14. **Know which emails not to delete.** I like to keep certain emails "just in case," such as emails that compliment or criticize your work product. Create folders and file away your emails so that you know where to find them if you need them in the future.

15. **Stay off the web.** Yes, everyone searches the internet while at work. But just like your email, big brother is watching. You are an adult, so I will assume I don't need to get into specifics on what's appropriate and not appropriate on your work computer (for the record, Pornhub will be caught every time and so will spending obsessive hours on Reddit, Pinterest, YouTube, etc.). I once worked in an office where an employee was printing pornography after-hours and he accidentally sent it to a printer room, which was locked, so he could not retrieve it. Guess who was fired the next day.

You've got to work like it's your first day on the job every day.
That's what I do. Work hard, laugh later.

-Nicki Minaj

16. **Be a team player**. I know it sounds cheesy, but most work environments involve a team in some form. Make sure you are always doing your part (even when others are not).

17. **Ask for feedback**. Most companies do annual performance reviews. However, depending on when you start, it may be quite some time before you receive one. In these instances, I suggest asking your boss for feedback on your performance after the first 90 days. They will be impressed that you asked and this will also give you an opportunity to correct any issues early.

18. **Don't look a hot mess if you have work travel**. I don't care if it's a weekend or early in the morning. When you travel for work, you are on the clock, so while you should dress comfortably, remember that you are working and representing the company. You never know who you may run into.

19. **Watch how much you drink at work events**. Even if the CEO gets wasted at the holiday party, it's not ok for you to do the same. It will take a long time to repair your brand from a drunken incident at a work dinner or party. Trust me—it's not worth it.

20. **Say yes to the extracurriculars**. Will you always want to hang out with your work colleagues after work hours? Probably not. But is it essential to do? Yes! It's called team building and developing relationships with your colleagues is important. So, don't be the be the one who always turns down requests to get together outside of work. Just don't forget tip #19.

TIP

At the time of writing this, 30 states and the District of Columbia currently have laws broadly legalizing marijuana in some form. Be aware that even if you live in one of these states, your employer can still have a zero-tolerance drug policy and your employment can be jeopardized by legal marijuana use.

---

21. **Take advantage of any professional development opportunities.** In the first few months on your new job, focus on doing your

job smart and well. Once you have mastered that, it's a good time to explore whether your company offers professional development benefits. Sometimes this will include paying for certain certifications or even classes on topics such as public speaking or software development. When the time is right, explore these benefits and take advantage of them. Not only will it help you grow professionally, but it will make you stand out as someone who is serious about their career and professional development.

22. **Understand company culture**. Some things about a company will just not be written down in the employee handbook. This is called *company culture* and is essentially the company's norms and habits (it's deeper than this, but hopefully this is enough to convey the idea). As a junior employee, it's important to understand the company culture and to do your best to align with it (unless, of course, it involves illegal or inappropriate activity). Let me give you a quick example, a friend of mine once received an email from a millennial employee that read:

> ***millennial mary****: hi dana, attached is the document you requested. let me know if you have any suggestions or questions.*
> ***Dana****: Where are your capital letters????*
> ***millennial mary****: this is how i typed at my last job. a study was conducted in the office that when you type in lower case without using the shift you are more "productive." little unknown interesting fact; however, i will type "correctly" if you would like.*

This is an example of not understanding company culture. Obviously, the culture in this office (and, frankly every office I've ever been in) was to use capital letters. Study or no study, this should have been recognized as a company norm, and the employee probably should not have tested out this new study with her boss.

23. **Navigate office politics.** Wikipedia defines office politics as, "the use of power and social networking within an organization to achieve changes that benefit the organization or individuals within it." Most people might say "Stay clear of office politics," but I advise you to navigate it *carefully*. It's not smart to engage in office politics, but you should be

aware of the players, the unwritten rules that may be in place, and move accordingly. It's my experience that it is better to be a quiet listener than an active participant.

24. **Gracefully exit when it's time to move on**. I know that we often have these grand images of throwing up the peace sign and telling our boss, "'I'm out!'". Before you do this, just know that this type of exit can follow you, especially in the early stages of your career. Be mature about your resignation, do it in writing, and offer a two-week transition timeline (i.e., two weeks' notice).

25. **Dress for the job you want, not the one you have**. Turn the page.

Dress for the job you want, not the job you have. Unless the job you want is Black Panther. Do not go to work as the Black Panther.

Chapter 4:

Appearance — It Actually Does Matter

You may be surprised that I am dedicating a whole chapter to appearance. I include it because it *does* matter and it *will* impact your long-term success. If it didn't, companies would not go through the trouble of issuing a dress code in employee handbooks. They do this because they want to ensure that the company's brand maintains a certain level of professionalism and decorum.

Also, not to point fingers, but this is an area where millennials specifically are challenged, because, much like hippies of the '70s, you are encouraged to express yourself through your clothing and style, and new trends are being driven through the power of social media. I've also found that millennials buck at the notion that they have to "conform" to what is considered *socially acceptable* and believe their appearance should not be a representation of who they are, blah, blah, blah.

While I'm not discounting any of this (ok, maybe I am just a little), the fact is: at work you are not being paid to do whatever you want. And, sorry to break it to you, that means if you want to get that paycheck, you will have to make sure your look represents the company brand during work hours. Here is how you

DON'T want the conversation to go when you are not around.

> **Your Boss' Boss (AKA the Big Boss)**: *Is Austin in yet?*
>
> **Your Boss**: *I haven't seen him. He may be running a few minutes late.*
>
> **Big Boss**: *Well, this may be a good time to share that I've received some comments about him wearing sweatpants to work. I don't know if he has looked around, but no one else around here is wearing sweatpants. Is he here to lounge around, or is he here to work?*
>
> **Your Boss**: *Actually, his work product is quite good, but I agree he probably could step up his attire.*
>
> **Big Boss**: *I don't care how great his work is, it's disrespectful that he is treating his job like it's his living room. I know you recommended him for the weekly CEO Lunch and Learn, but I refuse to have anyone in our conference room in sweatpants. I thought you would have spoken to him about this the first time it happened.*
>
> **Your Boss**: *I apologize, I should have already raised this with him, I will speak to him immediately.*

Big Boss: *If I see it happen again, he is out of here.*

This may sound like an extreme example but, trust me, it's not. First, Austin is late—his boss and boss' boss are already at work, and Austin is not. Second, Austin is rolling up to work in sweatpants. They could be Gucci sweatpants for all we know, but the fact remains that they are sweatpants, and Austin's brand is being perceived that he is too lazy to put on some real clothes (and get his butt to work on time!). Also, the sweatpants are a distraction from his work—which is apparently good, but the big boss doesn't care. Austin is also missing out on what could be some valuable face time with the CEO and could potentially lose his job over sweatpants.

Now, I know many of you may think that they can't fire Austin just because he has on sweatpants. WRONG. Most employment is "at-will," which, without getting all legal on you, means you can be terminated at any time without reason, explanation, or warning (AND you are free to quit at any time without reason). So, when it comes to dress code, unless you are being discriminated against, nine times out of ten an employer could fire you over some damn sweatpants. This is not legal advice—

just something to keep in mind when you wake up in the morning.

A good rule of thumb is to remember you are dressing for *work*, not for whatever you are doing before or after work. Sometimes, you may find an outfit that will work for both, but if you have to pick one over the other—dress for work and bring a change of clothes.

Also, every work environment is different— especially in today's workforce, and frankly the more casual the office, the trickier it can be to navigate what is appropriate and what is not. When you interview for a position, look around and check out what people are wearing in the office. Also, review the employee handbook and familiarize yourself with the dress code. If it's your first day and you have no clue what to wear, always err on the side of caution. Men wear a suit (with a tie) or slacks, collared shirt, and blazer (with a tie). If you are too over the top, you can always take off the tie and jacket. For women, I would advise the same thing (sans the tie) or a nice work-appropriate dress. DO NOT WEAR JEANS. Even if they are allowed in your office, save them for a few days after you really get to assess what the culture and dress code is of the office. Two true quick stories:

The first day of my very first real *adult* job was on Capitol Hill, which is suits and ties. The office I was going to be working in was moving into a new office space on the day I was starting. I was told I could wear jeans since I would be helping to move and unpack boxes. I thought long and hard about this. Should I really wear jeans on my first day on Capitol Hill (a place where jeans are usually a no-no?) And if I did not wear jeans, would it look like I did not know how to follow directions? Since I didn't know anyone in the office yet, there was no one to call or text to for advice (I don't even think I had a phone that could even send/receive texts at that time). So, I made the decision *not* to wear jeans. Instead, I wore black pants and a blouse and brought a pair of jeans with me. And guess what? When I showed up on that first day, no one had jeans on. The move had been delayed, and it was business as usual in the office. I would have stuck out like Taylor Swift at a Kanye West concert if I had shown up in jeans. The lesson here is to play it safe.

The second story is from another job on Capitol Hill. On my last day, my boss was thanking me for my work, and said, "I know this is going to sound strange, but thank you for always dressing appropriately." I laughed, and she continued, "No, I'm serious. I can't tell you how many young women I have to pull aside to coach on how to dress for work." She told me she appreciated that I took my job seriously and that I always looked the part (even though I was a low-level Hill staffer living in poverty). I told her I was always taught to dress for the job you want and not the one that you have. I wanted her job one day, so instead of dressing like the front desk girl, I dressed like the Chief-of-Staff (or the poor girl's attempt to dress like the Chief-of-Staff).

Without getting too preachy, this is my advice to you. Should your appearance count more than your work? Of course not. But people can be distracted by appearances and may not see that you are a high-performing employee because of your clothing style or grooming habits. I love fashion and I like to have fun with my clothes, hair, shoes, etc. I'm smart enough to know though that none of these things are possible without a paycheck to fund them, so over the years, I have made a point to always "look the part" at work. I want to look like someone who can be pulled into a last-minute meeting with a senior executive or lunch with the CEO. I want to look like someone who can represent the company at client meetings, conferences, trade shows—even if my job was to sit at my desk and answer the phones. I'm not saying you have to go out and rack up a credit card bill to look the part. What I encourage is for you to think of your appearance (from head to toe) as a part of the brand we talked about in the first chapter. It's important to think about what your boss and colleagues will say about it when you are not there. Should they be talking about your appearance? Probably not. Will they do it? Probably so. Therefore, let me give you some tips on how to put together an inexpensive but professional wardrobe. Again, every work environment will differ, but this is meant to give you a good idea of some key items that you should have to get off to the right start.

Women

1. My go-to shops for work attire are places such as TJ Maxx, Marshalls, Nordstrom Rack, etc. I am a dress person—and 4-5 sheath dresses can go a long way and are usually priced between $29.99-$49.99. For me, I like dresses because they are one-stop shop (no need to

match up a blouse and pants or a skirt) and you can mix them up with blazers and accessories.

2. If you are not a dress person, I would find a nice pair of black pants and buy 3-4 pairs of the same one (not a typo). One of the best investments I made when I was younger was a pair of black washable dress pants at Macy's (no dry cleaning needed!). I bought five pairs, and I wore them almost every day with different tops and accessories. The same goes for skirts—black is a safe color and you can repeat it without anyone taking notice.

3. Own at least one suit. I'm not a suit person, and while most jobs don't require you to be suited up every day, it's important to own at least one. I recommend a traditional one (grey, navy, or black are safe colors depending on your skin tone) that includes a pair of pants, skirt and blazer. I have not always had the best luck at TJ Maxx/Marshalls for suits, but Nordstrom Rack and Macy's usually have a good selection. And if the fit is not right, it's worth it to get it tailored. Yes, women need tailored suits too.

4. Get two pairs of nice work shoes. I know everyone is not into heels, but for me, having one pair of black heels and one pair of nude heels is a must. Also, keep them in good shape. Make sure they aren't scuffed—polish them if needed (this isn't just for guys) and please *please* don't ever wear your heels down to the metal tips. If you are a flats person—again find a nice pair—I personally believe that a patent leather flat is the best way to go.

5. Have a good work bag. It doesn't have to be fancy. I can usually find a nice size tote at TJ Maxx/Marshalls that can fit my laptop, notebook, etc.

Men

1. Own at least one suit that is tailored to fit you. It's better to have an inexpensive but decent quality suit that you get tailored than an expensive suit that you can't afford to tailor (if the quality is too low it may not be a good candidate for tailoring). Tip: Jos A Bank usually runs specials 5-6 times/year where guys can grab a suit for less than $300. An all-season

(preferably lined) wool suit is a good/safe choice.

2. Get 8-10 collared shirts on sale--enough to last you two weeks. Everywhere I go, I see men's dress shirts on sale. Find a deal and take advantage of it.

3. In addition to the collared dress shirts, it's also good to have on hand some polo shirts (both long sleeve and short sleeve, depending on the weather where you live).

4. Get a few pair of dress pants as well as khakis—and make sure to keep them in good shape and wrinkle-free. Also, wear a belt please. The workplace is not where you want to be asked to pull up your pants.

5. Start a tie collection and know how to tie them properly. There are a million videos on YouTube to help you learn how.

6. Get at least two nice pairs of work shoes— one of which should not have a rubber sole. Also, keep them in good shape—scuff free and polished as needed.

7. Have a good professional work bag. In some cases, this can even be a backpack, but I would upgrade it from whatever you carried in college.

Just Say No (at Work)

- Leggings
- Flip flops
- Clothing with words or a message
- Ripped jeans
- Visible bra straps
- Miniskirts
- Anything you would wear to a yoga class, the gym, the beach or da club

---

Beyond your clothes, also remember that good grooming goes a long way. I'm not anti-beard (even though I told my friend to shave his off for an interview), but facial hair should look like you give a damn. Long pointy nails are not usually appropriate in a conservative office environment, nor is purple and yellow hair, too much make-up, or strong cologne or perfume. I don't think work should prevent you from being you or suppress your inner style, but you should use your best judgment based on the environment. You don't want these irrelevant things to be a distraction from what you are seeking to achieve professionally. Is it fair? No, it's not. But as my mom has always said, no one ever said life was fair.

I'm hungry for knowledge.
The whole thing is to learn every day, to get brighter and brighter.
That's what this world is about.

-Jay-Z

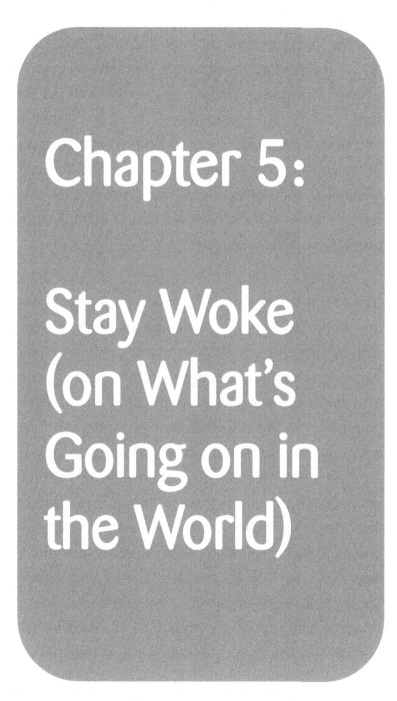

Chapter 5:

Stay Woke (on What's Going on in the World)

Often, millennials get labeled as a self-absorbed generation (remember I am a borderline millennial, so I get this all the time) and are perceived to be newsless, uninterested and disengaged from what's going on in the world. Some believe they are too caught up in producing the perfect social media feed that they have no idea what the hell else is happening around them (I know, all fake news).

As you navigate adulting, being able to have thoughtful conversations is now a necessity. Unlike in college, you are likely to come into daily contact with people who you may not think you have a lot in common with and probably have zero desire to chat it up with. Unfortunately, small talk is inevitable — whether it be about the weather, a popular book, or news story. I personally always love the look of surprise on someone's face when we unexpectedly connect on a random topic. This will especially be important in networking (covered in the next chapter) and it will also allow you to stand out in interviews as well as at work. This is why having some topics you can weigh-in on and contribute to in conversations is key. You don't want to be the person who is mute during these conversations because you have no idea what is going on in the world. The good news is that this is easy to do. The obvious medium to know what's going on is to watch the news, but here are a few other ways to be well versed in a little bit of "this" and a little bit of "that."

1. **News Podcasts**. I know some of you love podcasts and others have never even heard of them. I love them—free content that you can listen to on your phone? Sign me up! I highly recommend two daily podcasts that are available at 6am EST every weekday morning. Each give a quick run-down of key news to start your day in about 10 minutes— listen to it while you get dressed, eat your breakfast, walk your dog (my pick) or on your commute to work. The cool part is that before your work day starts, you will already be up to speed on the day's major news stories.

   - NPR Up First – 10 minutes of the top stories, from politics to pop culture.
   - The New York Times' The Daily – a 20-minute dive into a top news topic of the day.

TIP

Podcasts are also great for learning
more about your professional field
or other professional fields you have
interest in.

---

2. **Daily e-News**. If podcasts aren't for you, another great way to get a daily snapshot of relevant news is through an e-newsletter. A couple of my favorites are:

- Need2Know – a daily email with the news stories you 'need 2 know', from politics and business to sports and entertainment.

- The Skimm – This is a great newsletter to really dive into the news of the day in short, punchy paragraphs. Even though it's geared to female millennials, guys should not be scared away—news is unisex, right?

- PRSUIT – a daily email written for and by millennials that is "dedicated to helping you become your most badass self."
- Fast Company—I'm biased since it's one of my favorite magazines. They provide great newsletters on topics such as leadership, technology, money, creative people, etc. absolutely free (I subscribe to Leadership Daily).
- CNBC Morning Squawk – An early morning newsletter covering stock market news (it's not as boring as it may sound).
- Industry newsletters – Smart Brief and IndustryDive are two great platforms which produce a wide range of daily industry newsletters; find your industry and subscribe.

An investment in knowledge always pays the best interest.

-Benjamin Franklin

3. **LinkedIn.** In recent years, LinkedIn has taken on some features similar to other social media platforms. As you build out your connections, you will now have the option to scroll through a feed to read articles, blogs and other content posted by those in your network. Many of these posts are often related to business news, updates on your connections (for example you might stumble across an update that a connection just got a job at the same company where you are trying to get a job), and professional growth articles. These are good to check out in passing and also to repost and share with your network.

4. **Social Media.** I know millennials are starting to move away from the 'gram and Twitter, but for those of you still on it, I recommend adding a few news outlets or reporters to your feeds. CNN, MSNBC, Fox News, etc. all have active feeds and post news stories. Also, news networks are now starting to explore Snapchat—NBC has a twice daily new program on Snapchat called "Stay Tuned,"

and Snapchat produces its own news show called "Good Luck America."

5. **Google Alerts**. If you work in a specialty industry, another suggestion I will give you is to set up a google alert with keywords to stay on top of what's happening. For example, if you are working for a cybersecurity company or in healthcare, set up some alerts that send you industry news daily. You can pick and choose what is relevant and what you read. I also recommend setting up alerts for the name of the company or organization where you work (or want to be working). You don't want to be the last to know that the company is going out of business or introducing a new product or service.

6. **Books**. Yes, books—I know everyone is not a reader and many of you (myself included) struggle to find time for a good old-fashioned book. Books, however, are still a great information source and make for fantastic conversation topics. (Did you know that CEOs read an average of one book a week?) For those who can't fathom the idea of reading a hard copy book or from an e-reader, try out

listening to audiobooks.[9] I prefer to have an old-fashioned book in my hands, but that's just me. If an audiobook is the only way to get you through it, then do you, boo! Now, while I love a good mindless beach read, at this stage in your life, I highly recommend also reading books that propel your professional and personal growth. Books that may have been read by your colleagues or people that you might meet at a networking event are also good to keep in your rotation (One of my icebreaker questions is, "Have you read any good books lately?"). Here are three I recommend:

1. ***Who Moved My Cheese?* by Spencer Johnson, MD**. My mom gave me this book on my first solo travel adventure and it made me realize that living outside of your comfort zone is absolutely necessary. It's also a super quick and easy read.

---

[9] Don't forget you can download the audio version of this book for free at www.arikapierce.com.

2. ***Outliers* by Malcolm Gladwell**. I once overheard a group of college guys on a train from DC to NYC and they mentioned this book (in between asking how many girls each had slept with that semester). As I eavesdropped, I heard them say what a great book it was because it talked about why those who are most successful are outliers. I pulled it up on my Amazon app and ordered it immediately for both myself and my 20-year-old nephew. Great read!

3. ***Good to Great* by Jim Collins**. Not necessarily a quick read, and it can be very dense at times, BUT I guarantee that every great leader has read it. The first sentence says everything: "Good is the enemy of great." So, be great, and read the damn book.

TIP

If you haven't noticed, I love an app (it's the Xennial in me). I've recently come across an app called Blinkist. The app condenses nonfiction books into 15 minutes—basically a book report. I don't recommend this as the ONLY way to read, but I have to admit I love the concept. Note, Blinkist is about $8.00 a month and the book choices are so-so, but if you are looking to expand your knowledge library, it's worth it.

Keep up with the fun stuff too!

So, I don't want you to feel like that the only way to broaden your horizons is through news and books. At the end of the day, that does not make for a well-rounded individual. I encourage you to also explore other walks of life, cultures, hobbies, etc. For example, Netflix is a fantastic way to take yourself on a trip around the world, learn about some of the best restaurants, and even go back in time. Every now and then, check out one of the documentaries on a topic you know little to nothing about. I try to watch two to three a month. I've never been to Antarctica, but *Encounters at the End of the World* makes me feel like I have. I'm not a huge EDM music fan, but I have a new respect for Steve Aoki after watching *I'll Sleep When I'm Dead.* I thought I knew a decent amount about wine—but then I watched *SOMM.* You get the point—Netflix is a great way to expand your horizons from the comfort of your couch.

Also, if you have time, take classes, go to workshops, and always say yes when your boss or great aunt asks if you want tickets to the ballet, a museum exhibit, or a hockey game (even if you don't). The point is, be open to expanding your horizon beyond what you have been interested in forever. I love football and reality tv, but I am thankful that I have more depth than those two topics. I encourage you to form the habit of being open to new things because it will enrich life both personally and professionally.

Get into a habit of spending some time each day checking out what's going on around you. These days, it's fairly easy to get an overwhelming amount of information right from your phone. My recommendation is don't subscribe to everything and read/listen to nothing. Instead, pick a few information avenues that give you the type of news or information on topics that you are interested in in the format that works for you and roll with that. All of these sources are meant to ensure that you are smart, well-rounded and savvy. And yes, it will give you lots of topics to pick from when that small talk or big talk is needed.

TIP

Apps like Flipboard and Pocket are a great way to organize and save articles and website items you read online, or want to save and read later.

Surround yourself with the dreamers, the believers, the courageous, the careful, the planners, the doers, & the successful people with their heads in the clouds and their feet on the ground.

Chapter 6:

No New Friends Is Just a Rap Song

'm a huge Drake[10] fan, and when I'm out with my friends (or as Drake calls them my "dayones") and "No New Friends" comes on, I dance, point to my friends, and rap along to the lyrics about keeping your circle closed and tight. Well, I'm sorry to break it to you, this is just a song and is terrible advice for the real world. I have been blessed to continuously make new friends, acquaintances, mentors, etc. over the years. Do I have my core friends? Of course! But I also have been able to build some great new and diverse relationships which have propelled me to who I am today.

Just recently I met my old boss from my first job out of college (16 years ago!) to catch up. When I met him, I was a 21-year-old black girl who had just graduated from college, and he was a 40-something white man who, in all honesty, was intimidating, since it was my first job and he was my boss' boss. I don't mean to harp on our age and races, but what I want to express is that he was not someone who I thought I would ever have anything to talk about with, and at that time, I would have never guessed we would still be in touch so many years later. After

---

[10] Real name Aubrey

two years, when I left my first "real" job, he told me to keep in touch. And I did just that.

Over the years, he has become one of my biggest advocates, one of my mentors, and my friend. He's introduced me to new people, given me glowing job recommendations, and when I started my consulting firm, helped direct new clients to me. Had I not taken his initial advice and stayed in touch, my professional life would probably look quite different. The simple act of staying in touch and always being open to new friends has changed my life both personally and professionally. My advice to you is to do the same. If someone who may be a good go-to person in the future says "keep in touch," actually do it.

Create Your Own Board of Advisors

There is a great article published a few years ago in MIT's *Sloan Management Review* called "Assembling Your Personal Board of Advisors," (google the title and take the 20 minutes to read the article). It discusses how in today's world, checking the box and saying you have a mentor is no longer enough. Much like a CEO assembles a diverse group to advise him or her on running a company, as individuals we need a diverse team to develop us professionally and personally. Follow the advice of this article.

It's funny, I did not realize I had a board of my own, but I have always done my best to have different types of people in my circle to bounce ideas off who connect me with others and offer me sound advice. When I decided to quit my corporate job and start a consulting firm, if I only sought advice and guidance from someone who had worked at one company their entire life, they may have told me it was too risky and not to do it. Or when I decided to pursue law school and take on a huge amount of debt knowing I had no desire to practice law, I talked to lawyers, non-lawyers, as well as those who went to law school but did not practice. My point is that you need a variety of people, all who have different types of advice and life experiences to share, on your board of advisors. Don't just take this advice from me—there is MIT research to support this!

Because I know some of you still have not read the article, I'll do a short summary in my own words of the six types of personal advisors you need for your board.[11]

1. **Personal Guides**. This is not a day-to-day mentor and (especially in the world of social media, where we have lots of friends) it may not be someone who you even know personally. This is someone who inspires you. It could have been a teacher, a coach, or a boss. For me, this person has been Ursula Burns. I came across her name in 2009 when she became the first black woman CEO of a Fortune 500 company (Xerox). At the time, I was in my second year in corporate America and for the first time, truly experienced firsthand the lack of diversity in boss roles. I was inspired by Ursula Burns and her story of breaking glass ceilings, so much so that I kept a small picture of her (ok it was a poster) in my old office (yes I admit, slightly stalkerish).

---

[11] I think some of these categories overlap, which I note as well.

Dreams do come true, but not without the help of others, a good education, a strong work ethic and the courage to lean in.

-Ursula Burns

2. **Personal Advisors**. A personal advisor is a person (or people) who is always going to help make you a better you (professionally and personally). This may be a close personal friend or work colleague. I'm lucky enough that I have too many people in this category to name (my sister is always my number one supporter). These are people who genuinely support your constant quest for growth. For example, when I was in law school, instead of doing additional studying, I decided to compete in the Miss DC USA pageant to address deep-rooted self-esteem issues. Guess what? ALL of my true personal advisors did question the craziness of this (uh, shouldn't you be studying and not practicing how to pageant walk?). But they all still showed up and supported me. In the end, I gained self-confidence and learned how to start balancing my professional and personal life. I did not win.

3. **Full-Service Mentors**. These are your true-blue mentors. This person is likely older, has more experience and is your go-to on your life journey. Have more than one, and if possible, have at least one that does not work

with you—or if they work at your company they are not your boss. Remember that this person is helping you, so nurture and be proactive with this relationship. It's up to you to reach out to your mentor to catch up, share updates and/or ask to meet for coffee or dinner, etc. And you should be doing this actively and regularly.

4. **Career Advisors**. This is your go-to person for career advice. Sometimes it's your current boss, former boss, co-worker or former professor, etc. For me, these are the people who I only reach out to every now and then to bounce off career decisions. My former boss from 16 years ago who I referenced earlier, is one of my primary career advisors.

5. **Career Guides**. I honestly think a career advisor and guide are the same people in my life. That's all.

6. **Role Models**. The name speaks for itself. Always identify people who you admire (you may or may not know them). For me, Ursula Burns again rises to the top, but I also have other people whose work ethic I admire and strive to incorporate into my own.

This gives you a good summary of what your board of advisors should look like. Also, a person may serve in multiple positions. Some will evolve and change over time, and some will be with you 10, even 20 years from now. The point of this all is that you need a "really good team" (another Drake reference).

If you are new to the adulting world, you may not have people to fill these slots immediately. My advice to you is: from now until forever, keep and maintain your personal advisory board as you walk through life. If it helps, keep a running list of people who you have on your board or would like to have on your board. Check in with them periodically and let them know how things are going, especially at this dynamic time in your life. I have a list of about ten people. Periodically, I review the list and identify people I should check in with, people that should be removed, and people who should be added. I know it sounds a little over the top, but this is *your* board of advisors.

The opposite of networking is not working.

-Someone Smart

Networking 101

I will be the first person to tell you I *hate* networking. Whenever I say that, people laugh because I have to do it all the time professionally, and frankly I've been doing it long enough where I do admit I'm now good at it. Before I jump into tips, I recognize that some of you may have never attended a networking event or if, given a choice between networking and hanging out with your friends, your friends will win every time. So, let's do a quick dive into what networking is and why it's important.

As millennials, I recognize that networking through social media platforms is probably your method of choice. We already discussed the power of LinkedIn, so I'm not against it, but I will tell you that face to face networking still goes a long way. So first, what is networking? Some people will say it's the process of meeting new people and pretending to like each other while secretly strategizing how they can help your career. While there is some truth in this, a better way of thinking about it is relationship building based on work-related interests (as opposed to a love for cocktails or sports). Can real friendships be formed through networking? Absolutely! I met my old roommate at my first "adult" networking event and 15 years later, we are still friends.

Networking can occur anywhere and anytime, but for the purpose of this book, I am talking about networking events, receptions, panels, alumni events, etc. Anyplace where you have the opportunity to build new professional relationships. So, let's get to the tips.

1. **Do some ~~stalking~~ homework before the event**. Research the event and if possible, find out who will be there (sometimes an RSVP list might be published). Identify a few people who you are hoping to bump into. If you are feeling super aggressive, reach out to someone who will be attending and send a short note to introduce yourself, telling them that you hope to meet them in person at the event. (Warning: there is definitely a risk that this could be mistaken as a pickup line!)

2. **Create your own elevator speech**. What is your response if someone were to say, "Tell me about yourself." Be able to summarize who you are in 30-45 seconds.

3. **Target the right arrival time**. If the event has an open time frame, I don't like to be the first to arrive, but I don't like to arrive any later

then 30-40 minutes from the start time. Adults get just as cliquish as teenage girls. If you arrive too late, it will be challenging to break into conversations. If the event contains a program with speakers, be on time. You don't want to arrive in the middle of a program and have everyone looking at you.

4. **Set a goal of meeting at least three new people at an event.** I'll be honest, once I meet my goal of three (unless there is something keeping me there), I'm usually out. One piece of good advice I have received is whenever you are ready to leave, stay an additional fifteen more minutes.

5. **Step up to the singles.** Not the single girls and guys, but the people who are also walking around aimlessly hoping that someone will save them. My never-fail line is to go up to this person and ask, "What brings you here?" This will usually spark a response that gives you something to work with. Other good openers are, "Have you been to events like this before?" or even "How's your day going?" Also, once the ice is broken, LISTEN.

6. **Mix and mingle and mix some more.** Sometimes it's easy to get stuck talking to one person and sometimes it's easier to just talk

with the same person (especially if you already know them) verses working the room. Keep in mind your goal of meeting three new people and know that it's ok to politely exit a conversation. I often say, "It was great to meet you! I'm going to walk around a little bit more before I head out." At this time, if it makes sense, ask for their card, share yours if you have one, and/or suggest you connect on LinkedIn.

7. **Don't be afraid to join a convo.** I know, it feels completely awkward and for me, it gives me flashbacks to my elementary school cafeteria. I remind myself that 99% of the people at the event are there to meet new people. My approach is to walk up to the group and say, "Hi, do you mind if I join you?" No one has ever told me no (promise).

8. **Exchange info with (almost) everyone you meet.** In my day (kidding, I'm not that old!), exchanging business cards was the best way to way to keep in touch. However, you may not have cards or work for a company that views business cards as a waste of paper. In these cases (and sometimes even when I have business cards), I like to ask for the other person's email address and email them on

the spot a short email—*Hi Jack, It was great to meet you at (event name). My contact info is below—let's connect soon.*

TIP

If you do take someone's card, make a note on their card of something you talked about, any follow-ups (i.e., a promise to send an article), or anything that will help you remember who that person is. It can be as simple as "guy in the weird shirt who is about to launch a drone startup and is looking for programmers." This will help you later on when you have a stack of business cards and are struggling to remember who is who.

---

9. **Follow-up**. If you sent an email while you were still at the event, you are already ahead of this step. If you have a business card or contact info, I would suggest sending an email in the next 1-2 days (same as above). Also,

connecting on LinkedIn is a good idea and *maybe* on Twitter if they have a professional non-private page. I stay away from Facebook, IG, and Snapchat for professional contacts.

10. **Schedule lunch, coffee, etc., at least once a month**. Ok, so you have suggested that you connect soon with your new contact. Now actually do that. Take time each month to reach out and invite someone to a coffee, lunch, drink, or another event that they might be interested in. This is how you start to build your professional network. Remember, someone may not be a right fit for your network, but they may know others who they can connect you with (and vice versa). You will be surprised at the huge value that meeting new people can bring. The goal here is to build a network before you need anything. So be friendly and get to know new people.

11. **STAY OFF YOUR PHONE**. If you are at an event, keep in mind your reasons for being there. It will be very difficult to meet new people if you are constantly scrolling through your IG feed, texting, or Snapchatting from the event. It's ok to bring your phone out for

information exchanges, but outside of that, stay off your phone while you are there.

As much as I'm not a fan of the phrase, "It's not what you know; it's *who* you know," there is a lot of truth in it. Making a new connection, building out your board of advisors and becoming a master networker are all important pieces of the adulting puzzle. To be clear, I am <u>not</u> suggesting that you go out and create a bunch of superficial and fake relationships to advance your career. I am recommending that you expand your circle beyond the group of friends you had in college or high school. The reason for this is that they are likely to look like you, be around the same age as you and know many of the same people that you know. By opening yourself up to a more diverse group of acquaintances, friends, advisors, mentors, etc., you will grow as a person and be exposed to and challenged at different levels.

For me, without some of the people I've known over the years, I would have missed out on many amazing opportunities that have benefited me both personally and professionally. Make new friends. Trust me on this one.

ASSIGNMENT

Identify an upcoming networking event and commit to meeting three new people. Start a list of 5-6 people who you would like on your personal board of advisors.

What would you do if you were not afraid?

-Spencer Johnson, MD *Who Moved My Cheese?*

Chapter 7:

Jumping In Is the New *Lean In*

n 2013, Sheryl Sandberg, the Chief Operating Officer at Facebook (pre-Facebook being taken over by your parents) wrote a book that got a lot of attention called *Lean In*. The book was written for women. It discussed the ways women are held back in the workplace due to gender differences and how women hold themselves back due to reasons such as lack of self-confidence. I have to admit, when I read the book it changed the way I approached different situations at work and I have consciously coached myself to *lean in* throughout the years.

That being said, many of the themes in Sandberg's book as well other books, articles, and blogs that have been written on the same topic are not just good advice for women. It's great advice for anyone who may not feel confident in the workplace due to reasons such as age, ethnicity or level of experience. My advice is to forget about leaning in. In this day and age, leaning is not enough. So, let's JUMP IN.

Jump
/jemp/
verb

1. To push oneself off a surface and into the air by using the muscles in one's legs and feet.

2. To move suddenly and quickly in a specified way.

Think about all the crazy and fearless things that require jumping—jumping out of a plane, bungee jumping, cliff jumping, etc. These are all adrenaline-laced activities that are primarily done by thrill seekers and risk takers. While I'm not advocating for (or against) any of these, I encourage you to be a person that someone is willing to take a risk on. This can be interpreted a lot of ways, but for now, I am talking specifically professionally. For me, there has never been a better feeling than when my boss has asked me to take on a project that they knew would challenge me. I accepted the challenge, and I killed it. Now don't get me wrong, I recognize that it's not normal to go looking around for extra work or to be the first one to volunteer for a project that you know is going to requiring working late or over a weekend. But remember, the goal here is to rise above the labels of normal or average. Strive to be extraordinary, stellar, epic, dope, Gucci, or whatever word describes that you are not like the others. Lots of people will make judgments about your capabilities and work ethic given the fact that you are a millennial. It's not fair, but unfortunately, there are so many that fall into this negative stereotype that it makes it hard to prove it wrong. So, JUMP IN! Show that *your* brand is one that is always ready to take on new challenges (even if you are not sure you are completely ready).

If you're offered a seat on a rocket ship, don't ask what seat. Just get on!

-Sheryl Sandberg

For me, public speaking has always been a fear. I felt I lacked experience and the self-confidence needed to captivate a crowd and sound *smart* while doing so. In 2008, I took my first management level role and almost immediately, my boss asked me if I felt comfortable enough to present the strategic plan for my department in front of not just my boss but also the President, CEO, and about 100 employees. When I tell you that I freaked the F out, *I freaked the F out.* I actually thought to myself, "What is my boss thinking, asking little ole me to give this type of presentation?! Shouldn't this be something that she is better fit to do?!"

I was afraid that the President and CEO would hear two minutes of me presenting and wonder why the hell I was hired. I wanted to decline the opportunity and say I wasn't ready yet, but I knew that wasn't actually an option. Long story short, I agreed to do it, and then googled "How to present a strategic plan." I over prepared and I rehearsed as if I was about to give the State of the Union address. I was nervous, but I got through it and I killed it. I then went on to become someone in the company who was regularly asked to present not just at internal meetings but conferences as well.

Public speaking has now become something that I'm pretty good at and I actually enjoy doing it. However, if I said no when I was first asked, or even hesitated, my boss would probably have waited a long time before asking me to do something challenging again. Worse, she would have labeled me as someone who could not *jump in* and take on new challenges. Think about all of the singers and rappers who have only 30 seconds notice to perform for a big music executive to possibly get their big break. There is no, "Can you give me a day or two to get back to you?" The work environment is your stage. Shine bright like a diamond at all times. Here's how:

1. **Have a voice.** I spent my early years in my corporate career afraid to have a voice in meetings, on conference calls, or generally at work. I worried people would think whatever I had to say was uninformed, unintelligent, or pointless. Then, I learned that you don't want to be the person who no one ever hears speak. Silence can project the image that you are not engaged or are disinterested. There is a fine line in how to do this right and there are times when it is best to keep your mouth

shut—especially when you are in an entry-level position. In general, try to add a comment here or there, ask a question or, when also else fails, affirm something that someone has already said ("That's a great point, Mark!"). You can't jump in if you are invisible. The next time you are afraid to share ideas, remember someone once said in a meeting, "Let's make a film with a tornado full of sharks."[12]

2. **Don't be afraid of new opportunities.** Hopefully, my earlier story was convincing enough. I urge you to raise your hand, be out in front, and say yes to any opportunity that will take you to the next level or raise your visibility (ok, not "any" opportunity—use your best judgment). Many times we let fear, insecurities and just plain laziness stand in our way. My answer to that is if your dreams don't scare you, then they are not big enough (said by the great Muhammed Ali). I see so many people not apply for new jobs or a promotion because they think they are not qualified or ready. I have breaking news: There are people who run for President of the

---

[12] There are now five *Sharknado* films.

United States (and win!) who may or may not be qualified, and that doesn't hold them back! The only way to make your mark is to jump in and give it your all. Yes, there is a chance you may get in over your head, but if you manage it appropriately, it is all part of the learning process.

I once asked my boss if I could work part-time in a completely different department (in addition to a full-time job) to get some new experience. It was a disaster. There was too much work and I didn't even like the work I'd piled on my plate. I stuck it out for 90 days and then went back to my boss and explained that while I enjoyed the experience, it reaffirmed my commitment and interest in my current position. And you know what? It was not the end of the world and I think she respected that I wanted to expand my skillset and take on a new role. I tried it out and learned a lot, but knew it wasn't for me. I had the courage to let her know it wasn't working out and to keep it moving.

3. **Don't Be Afraid to be Your Own Hype (Wo)Man.** In the early stages of your career, it's easy to wait to be given what's owed to

you. And to be honest, millennials get a bad rap for coming off as though they are owed everything and don't work for anything. All this being said, you are now at a stage where, to get ahead, you *must* promote yourself. Can this be tricky? Yes. And I'm not talking about running around boasting about your best qualities at all times. Rather, it's about making sure the right people are aware of your best qualities at the right time.

If you see an opportunity that you want to go after, ask for it and be ready to make a case for why. I've learned over the years that no one will advocate for me better than I do. No one can tell my story, explain my experience, or promote myself the way that I can. The bottom line is that you cannot wait to be noticed or be too modest at times. Yes, there will always be people who seem to get presented with amazing opportunities that allow them to move to the next level in life, and then there are the rest of us who have to jump in and promote ourselves to capture that opportunity. Strive to be the latter.

That horrifying moment when you are looking for an adult, but realize you are an adult. So, you look around for an *adultier* adult.

Chapter 8:

CONGRATS! You Are Officially Responsible for Your MIND, BODY, & ~~SOUL~~ FINANCES

Most of this book has focused on transitioning into adulting professionally. While there is so much more I could have added in every chapter, I intentionally chose to focus on the topics that rose to the top. This last chapter focuses on some of the personal transitions to adulting and how to take care of the most amazing person you know—yourself! None of the seven previous chapters matter if you don't take care of yourself and to be honest, I have seen so many people (including myself) learn this the hard way. Life as a full-fledged adult can be super overwhelming and frankly, the carefree nature of college will definitely be missed, but you have to keep it moving. For me, there are three checkpoints that drive my sanity: my mind, my body, and my finances.

Mind

I am not a mental health expert, but I take mental health VERY seriously and I don't think it gets enough attention. Many are often surprised to know I have struggled with depression over the years and that sometimes I wish I could have daily instead of weekly sessions with my therapist (unfortunately, I cannot afford this). I have often struggled to find true happiness as an *adult* no matter how much I fake it. As you start to move around this thing called adult life, my advice to you is to make sure that you check in with yourself mentally. Ask yourself if you are happy and if you are not, start thinking about the ways you can get there. Be willing to try different things that will strengthen you mentally, such as meditation or yoga. Seek out your passions, create vision boards, pray, read motivational books, etc. Everything isn't for everybody. But we all want to be happy and there are tools that can help get us there.

A few years ago, I was going through a tough time and was tired of feeling sorry for myself for no reason. The holidays were approaching, and I decided that I needed to channel my energy into something that was greater than and more important than me. I booked a mission trip to Haiti that left the day after Christmas and came back in the New Year. I recognized mentally that this would get me out of my funk (and it was truly a funk), refocus my negative energy into something positive, and help others at the same time. It worked, and I came back in the new year refocused and reenergized. Does everyone need to run out and book a trip to a third world country? No. But do take your mental fitness seriously, and find ways to maintain your happiness. Here're a few ways to do so.

1. **Listen to motivational talks**. Guess what? YouTube is filled with some great talks. Now, I don't mean just regular people ranting into their iPhone and posting (though some of these can be quite profound as well). I am talking about professional motivational speakers. I listen to a lot of TedTalks. I usually find a good one and then YouTube will list other talks on similar topics. I then stream the talks on my Echo while I do laundry or clean the kitchen. Two of my favorites are: *Everyday Leadership* by Drew Dudley and *Get Comfortable with Being Uncomfortable* by Luvvie Ajayi. Also, podcasts are another great place to find some great motivational talks. Oprah's *Super Soul Conversations Podcast* is always a good choice when you need some words of wisdom.

2. **Unplug**. Look, I get it. If you are like me, your cellphone is like a pacemaker. I go to

bed with my phone. I wake up to it. I have a mild panic attack if, for 30 seconds, I think I have lost it. Unfortunately, our phones and social media can impact us negatively. When it does, recognize it and unplug. For example, if I feel like I'm going too far down the *everybody's life looks better than mine* rabbit trail on Instagram, I delete the app from my phone for a few days. Our phones have turned into something they were not intended to be, and they can drive us crazy—literally. Know when to pull the plug.

3. **Create a Vision Board.** I am a big believer in creating vision boards so that you can visually see what you want for your life. I've done one at the end of each year for about 7-8 years now and can attest that they work. My friends and I have vision board parties (what's a vision without wine?) and we present them to each other because we all must be comfortable with sharing and speaking what we want into existence. This is a time in your life when it's so easy to get off track and to feel lost, unsure, and overwhelmed by changes in

your career, your friendships, family dynamics, relationships, etc. I wish I had started doing vision boards much earlier in life. Even if you think the notion of it is cheesy (and some men may think of it as a "girl" thing to do, but goals and vision have no gender), it does force you to take time to think about what it is you want to happen in your life. This alone can do wonders for you mentally. If you can see it, you can believe it.

4. **Read.** I am an avid "buyer" of self-investment books (sounds better than self-improvement). Some I read cover to cover and some I just keep around and pick up as needed. Here are a few of my go-to's:

   - *The Four Agreements: A Practical Guide to Personal Freedom* (short book, stays on my nightstand so that I can read over and over again)
   - *The Power of Focus: How to Hit Your Business, Personal and Financial Targets with Absolute Confidence and Certainty* (Recently read this. Every chapter has action steps and drives

you to make positive and productive changes in your life)

- *You Are a Badass: How to Stop Doubting Your Greatness and Start Living an Awesome Life* by Jen Sincero I saw everyone reading this bright yellow book with "BADASS" on the cover and bought a copy. It has definitely motivated me to start taking action on making my dreams come true.

- *Get Your Sh*t Together: How to Stop Worrying About What You Should Do So You Can Finish What You Need to Do and Start Doing What You Want to Do* by Sarah Knight (Bought this book in the airport based on the title alone. Great read, and yes it really did help me get my sh*t together).

- *The Millennial's Playbook to Adulting* by Arika L. Pierce (I know the author well, great gift for all of the millennials you know).

5. **Journal.** Confession: I am awful at journaling. I'll do it for a few days and then fall right off and won't pick it back up for months (or years). One thing I have learned (through therapy) is to not be so hard on myself. Journaling is cathartic, and it's ok to do it as needed. One thing I do try to hold myself accountable for is a gratitude journal, and most recently I've discovered a journal called the Five-Minute Journal.[13] Also, journaling does not have to be pen to paper—it can be done on your phone.

6. **Find a healthy outlet.** At this time in your life, it's very easy to get overwhelmed (I know, I keep saying this) and feel like you are losing control. Before this happens, identify a healthy outlet or something that you like to do to channel some of this nervous/anxious energy. Some people like to paint, others like to make music and some like to bake. Whatever it is, find something healthy that you can do when you need a release. I emphasize health

---

[13] Check it out at www.intelligentchange.com

because going to happy hour with your friends is sometimes what we need after a bad or long day, but isn't always the healthiest option to turn into a habit, so think of something that doesn't involve alcohol, drugs or glutinous amounts of food.

7. **Make a happy list.** Think about the things that make you feel most happy and make a list of them (if you can, try to list 50-100). My list includes: working out, laughing with my girlfriends, feeling productive at work, traveling, good hair days, 100% battery life. Go to the list when you are feeling down and need a boost.

8. **Know when to get help.** I would be remiss if I didn't say that you can do all of these things and more, but sometimes you need professional help. I've already shared that therapy is critical for me and my peace of mind. I recognize that therapy is not for everyone, but don't be embarrassed about it and don't be afraid to seek it out. I personally don't know why people are so ashamed or embarrassed to be in therapy. Few people are

embarrassed or hide when they hire a personal trainer and I don't see the difference.

ASSIGNMENT

Create a vision board. It doesn't matter that it's not January 1st—your vision for the future can start today!

Body

OK, the mind is covered, now let's get down to the body. I recognize that you probably did not buy this book to get fitness tips (and I have none to give). But what I will tell you is that many reading this book are at an age where you may think you are physically invincible and I'm here to tell you: that is simply not true for anyone who is alive (if you are reading this my assumption is that you are).

Since I left college and had to start taking care of myself, the body-maintenance part has been a challenge. It's now up to you to hold yourself accountable for a lot of things you did not have to worry about before. Here are things I have learned:

1. If you have insurance, go to the doctor. If you don't have insurance, get some ASAP (if you are under 26, your parents can still cover you).

2. Schedule physical and annual visits around your birthday so that you always know when it's time for a check-up.

3. Listen to your body. If something doesn't seem right, see #1.

4. Learn to cook something. Uber Eats, GrubHub, Postmates, etc. get expensive and basic cooking is a survival skill.

5. Eat something healthy (at least from time to time). The days of Chipotle and Chick-fil-A everyday do not make for a healthy mind, body or spirit. You may not be ready to dive head first into brussels sprouts and kale shakes, but starting to eat things that are not featured on the kid's menu is not a bad thing.

6. Work out (your metabolism will soon leave you for a younger person and it also does wonders for your mental health)

7. Don't go broke working out (no gym requires you to wear Lululemon or Under Armour).
8. Watch the alcohol intake. At some point, your recovery time will not be what it used to be and the empty calories will catch up with you.
9. Get enough sleep.
10. Drink A LOT of water. Just a friendly reminder.

My favorite childhood memory is not paying bills.

Finances

No playbook on the transition to adulting would be complete without touching on the dreaded F word—finances! Also, known as money, coins, paper, Gs—or whatever is your choice word. If you thought it was hard to manage money before, you have not seen anything yet. I am the furthest thing from a financial advisor and learning to manage my finances as an adult challenged me for a long time. My financial theory was: as long as the card doesn't get declined all is well in my personal finance world.

It took me a long time to start taking my money seriously, to stop wasting money on silly stuff, to start saving, investing, and to understand what was coming in money-wise and what was going out. I recently came across a great book called *Money Honey: A Simple 7 Step Guide for Getting Your Financial $hit Together* by Rachel Richards (the title alone spoke to me!)[14]. It's one of the best books I have read about personal finance, and it's written for millennials. She covers everything from debt, investing, taxes, insurance and even creating a personal money strategy. While you wait for her

---

[14] Available on Amazon

book to arrive, here are my top tips on ways to not go broke!

1. **Budgets are for everyone.** I'll be honest—I created my first real budget last year. Before that, I would always say, "budgets are not really my thing." I honestly thought that as long as I didn't overdraw any of my accounts and put some money in savings that there was no reason to have a budget. What I have since learned is that budgets come in different flavors (just like vodka). You just have to pick the one that works best for you. Some people need a very strict budget where they track every penny to prevent overspending. Others do better working to meet a specific savings goal. I put myself in the "I just want to live within my means" category, so my goal is to have a general idea of how much I am spending and make better-informed decisions on purchases (I was shocked to see my monthly Uber bills are sometimes around $500 per month, that's a whopping $6,000 a year AND I own a car!!). Just figure out what kind of budget you need and spend an hour or so each month

checking out your spending. It's a good habit to get into to now—and will only help you in the long run.

TIP

There are LOTS of apps to help you manage your money. I use one called MINT that is free, easy to set up, and gives quick visibility into your spending. Another good one if you are working towards a savings goal is YNAB (You Need a Budget). Unfortunately, it's not free ($6.99/per month), but it has some really cool features that go a step further than MINT.

---

2. **SAVE something**. I know it's a no-brainer, but it's worth stating. Your days of calling your parents, other relatives, and friends to bail you out start to get numbered as you move into adulthood. It is possible to lose your job

overnight and losing your job means losing your income. It happens all the time, especially in today's economy. Also, unplanned expenses will pop up, like car repairs or emergency trips to Vegas after a breakup (kidding, kind of). The rule of thumb is to usually have enough in your savings to cover three months worth of living expenses. Yes, this can be a lot. But figure out how much you can put away each paycheck, even if it's just $25, and set up your direct deposit to send that amount automatically to your savings account each pay period. This way, that money doesn't even get a chance to co-mingle with your "spending" money. I actually have a separate savings account at a completely different bank than my checking account to keep it separate. My checking and savings do not hang out together.

3. **Say yes to your 401K.** If your company offers a 401K retirement savings, try to contribute something to it, especially enough to trigger your employer's match. I know retirement seems a world away right now, but starting to save now is a good habit to get into. I

understand if you are in a place where you need every penny because I was there for most of my 20s. But when the time is right, say yes and don't leave your employer's money on the table.

4. **Watch your credit score.** A lot of us have learned this the hard way, including me. Pay your bills on time, don't let your credit situations get out of hand and stay on top of your credit score. In *Money Honey,* Rachel calls your credit score a GPA for your finances, and it's so true. As you know, it takes a lot to maintain a high GPA and a single bad grade can mess it up. Think of your credit score the same way. Like your 401K, it may not seem important right now, but one day you may want to buy a house, car, or anything that requires a line of credit. If your credit score sucks, you will be screwed—it takes seven to ten years to get anything bad off of your credit report.

5. **Educate yourself on investing.** When I was in my 20s, I didn't know anything about investing. Frankly, my goal at the time was to keep my checking account from overdrawing, so it was not a top priority for me. I now know

that even if you don't have the money to invest, it's still smart to understand it, to watch the stock market, and to be financially literate about investment opportunities as a whole. While the stock market is not for everyone, it can be a way to increase your income (If you invested $1,000 in Netflix 10 years ago, it would now be worth over $50,000). If you aren't yet ready to invest your money in the market, it is interesting to watch what drives a company's stock price up and down. Also, some people think you have to be "rich" to invest in the stock market. Not true. My recommendation is to plug a few companies that you like into the stock market app on your phone and start to follow their daily, weekly, or monthly changes. Then, when you are ready to open up a brokerage account (it's not as scary as it sounds), you'll have a better idea of where you want to invest. I like the Robinhood app, which is very popular for millennials because there are no-fees to trade (other sites charge on average $7).

DJ Khaled recently partnered with
Weight Watchers and will be using his
social media platforms to share his
weight loss using the program.
Shares of Weight Watchers
went up 9%.

---

6. **Diversify your income.** Even if you are not
ready to increase your income through the
stock market, always be thinking about other
ways to (legally) make money outside of your
day job. To be honest, this comes very easily
to millennials due to the entrepreneurial
spirit of the millennial generation, as well as
the constant desire to automate and disrupt
everything. I believe it's important to have
multiple and diverse income streams, even if
you have your dream job and are making tons
of money. My only advice is always make sure
your side gig does not conflict or interfere
with your primary income. Some companies
have restrictions on outside work, but most
don't completely prohibit it. To be on the safe

side, google the article "How to Avoid Getting Fired When Starting a Side Business" by Ryan Robinson.

Way to Diversify Your Income

- Drive for Lyft/Uber
- Dog walking
- Sell old clothes on Poshmark
- Open an Etsy store
- Join the gig economy

---

7. **Understand your debt.** When many of you left college, you left it with student loan and credit card debt. You may also have other debt, like a car loan. Whatever it is, start tracking it now and continue to track it. Update the chart when you take on new debts and remove paid-off debts. I keep mine in one spreadsheet with the following columns: loan name, payoff balance, interest rate, monthly payment, # of payments, and total of payments. This allows me to know at all times, where I am from a debt perspective,

which is key info for making any financial decisions.

8. **Create smart money habits.** Again, I am not a financial expert, but if there is one thing I hope you take away from this final section is the importance of being smart with your money. One of the most challenging parts of adulting is money. Unless you are one of the lucky ones, it may be a long time before you have enough of it (and in the words of Lil Wayne, "too much money ain't enough money"). So until this happens, be aware of your money habits. Late fees on bills add up, you may not need every subscription box or sometimes taking the Uber pool may be the better choice. Automatic renewal subscriptions are not always a good thing, and yes, it's sometimes worth walking an extra three blocks to your home bank to avoid that $3.50 ATM fee. Be smart with your money, or alternatively, create an app where money does grow on trees (I'll be the first investor!). Tip: One of the best text messages I get everyone morning is from Bank of America reporting my checking account balance (ok, maybe it's not the best text I get, but it's the most "responsible" text I get). It

helps me stay on track of how much cash I have on hand (and confirms that my account is not overdrawn!).

ASSIGNMENT

Inventory your spending over the past three months. How much did you spend on happy hour? Uber/Lyft? Fast food?

Create a debt spreadsheet.

Identify 3-5 stocks to start tracking

Conclusion

YES!! You read to the end. I'll keep this short.

As I said in the introduction, my goal for writing this book was simple. I wanted to give millennials a one-stop shop for straight-up advice to help make the transition to adulting easier. I have had some missteps over the years and would have loved for someone to have handed me a book breaking down some of these topics. For whatever reason, there seems to be a disconnect between millennials and previous generations, and millennials are sometimes not given a fair chance. We have all been shaped by all kinds of factors, and all us could use a playbook on life. If you are reading this, I am thrilled that you have made it to the end of the book. I truly hope there was something in these pages that you will carry with you and will help guide you through your adulting journey.

5 Final Asks

Please
1. Share this book with anyone who would benefit from it.
2. Follow me on social media.
3. Email or tweet me, and tell what you thought about the book.
4. Take two minutes to write a quick review on Amazon.
5. BE THE BEST DAMN ADULT YOU CAN BE!!!

Where to find me

Instagram: @themillennialsplaybook

Facebook: @themillennialsplaybook

Twitter:　@themillennialPB

Email:　hi@arikapierce.com

Website:　www.arikapierce.com

and so the adventure begin.....

Made in the USA
Coppell, TX
26 August 2021

61034161R00095